To Spin the Universe Golden

To Spin the Universe Golden

Poems by
Adira Naidu

First published in 2020 by Annalese Press
134 Towngate
Netherthong
Holmfirth
West Yorkshire HD9 3XZ
England

Copyright © 2020 Adira Naidu

All rights reserved. No part of this publication may be reproduced, stored, or transmitted in any form, or by any means electronic, mechanical or photo-copying, recording or otherwise, without the express written permission of the publisher.

Cover design by Peter Wadsworth

British Library Cataloguing-in-Publication Data
A catalogue record for this book is available on request from the British Library.

ISBN 978-1-9163620-0-0

For my mother

Contents

When the ochre sunrise	1
If rare tinted damask	3
My mother worries for me	4
In a world of arranged shoes	6
In the season of monsoons	7
When we moved here	9
Why do I wait for you	11
When Krishna comes for me	12
What will become of us	13
In February	15
In the garden	16
When my brother passed his exam	18
My mother tells me	20
My father's voice is a soft wing	21
For the meal	23
The crescent moon	24
I have lived here	25
Shiva	27
You spread seed	28

Harvest time	30
In the grove of sacred trees	31
Around my neck	33
Off in the distance	34

Dark Friend, what can I say
this love I bring
from distant lifetimes is ancient
do not revile it.
Seeing your elegant body
I am ravished.
Visit our courtyard, hear the women
singing old hymns
On the square I've laid
out a welcome of teardrops,
body and mind I surrendered ages ago

taking refuge
wherever your feet pass.
Mira flees from lifetime to lifetime
your virgin.

Mirabai

When the ochre sunrise

kneels like a crush
in my tired eye

I peel the skin
of my father's lost table
imagine him five years old
making cakes for the festival
his mother soaking the dates
rolling thin the sweet dough

imagine him before the long journey
that took him away.

Here I wait with no wings.
The streets hold plastic dolls
car parks the size of a lake.
Their gods do not speak to me.

I say prayer
call back the ancestors
paint the combed sleeves
of the dark
red with lotus.

If rose tinted damask

was the heavy weight
color of my love

would you forgive
my trials
petty invocations

see me as novitiate

in the dwindled kingdom
the one with a twig stick
who scratches the dirt
calls Ganesha home
atop his mouse throne

would you look favorably
not place me in a metal box
with dead ants?

My mother worries for me

as if I have forgotten
the goddess who swims
in the holy river

have let my hands fail

but I know you are the tree
of my longing
that lives secret
in the soul's chamber

the one who calls
when the night holds daggers
when stars are a dice roll

that you sweep my room
wait
will not give up

as if every meal
I have ever prepared
ever eaten
is your secret tribute.

In a world of arranged shoes

my parents hold snug to their hearts
won't let their love turn cold
drizzle.

Like the mahogany tree
my sister and brother grow tall
erect on their words.
I try to grow tall, straight
but a woodsman comes
chops down half my branches.

Now I am a remainder of
torn limbs
but nobody sees this
my shrunken and dry rot

tilted house
how a thwarted girl
can prevail.

In the season of monsoons

it is hard to live on the street
sleep under tarps, cardboard
yet people look after each other
share sandals, kindling, food, pots
consolation, laughter.

Here we have a house on a tidy road
fenced yard, dog, pear tree
here my mother has pots and pans
sorrel in the garden
rooms for her children

here my father travels by car
makes decent pay
crosses miles where nobody listens

here we memorize history, words
memorize awards, success
memorize concrete, plastic

here the neighbors stay indoors
our uncles and cousins turn distant

I weep and sing
weep and sing

for what we've lost
what might become of me.

When we moved here

I was too young to know different
drank in the light
the roadway, box stores

learned to make myself an enterprise
like everybody else.
Kali the girl with the pearled smile
never absent from school
never naughty
good at school band

girl who dissects frogs
memorizes words
wins the regional spelling bee
makes her parents' proud
a room of framed trophies

learns to eat hot dogs, fries, relish
soft serve buried in sprinkles

learns to keep that other life
away from school, her friends
secret.

Why do I wait for you

in the garden
as if my life is a flat throne
eager to lift

heart shaped leaf
of the Peepal tree
longing to be snatched up
in your wind's empire
spin.

When Krishna came for me

I was not yet willing
too young to know
the cost of courtship
too soon to spend my lips
on his blue seduction

but still he waits
serenades with flute
among the marigold

offers up hibiscus, musk roses
almond

as if I am more than
the crooked light
beggarly

carry the stars
in my soul.

What will become of us

a nation of nomads
saffron and lotus and mud
parched crops
lost homeland

where will we go
when we lose our way
the gods desert us

what will we do
when the night rustles
her silken robe
nobody listens?

I tend a fire you can't see
am not sure I know
how to name things.

In the night's shrunken sleeve
a pale moon stalls at my window
Krishna plays flute
Parvati dances
for her I comb my hair silken
and for my mother
whose own life
is a silver stained river
of distances.

In February

when the dust settles
the sunbird travels away

when the cracked earth offers up
small bones
lost keys

I memorize your graffiti
saffron

ink my hands
in the forgotten language
the wind's wet lips
trees' tutelage

as if nothing offends.

In the garden

my mother gathers prayer
potatoes, peas
fills her basket
swabs the curled ends of her life
so that nothing goes missing

and if she lives like a torn branch
in a foreign landscape
she is not saying

recounts stories of home
her father plucking
the strings of his sitar
she and her sisters silent
listening.

Her hair sways long, black
ribboned with silver
an unsoiled river
anchored up with a turquoise clip.

Out in the yard
my mother gathers yams
mint, onion
her back a soft curve
quiet song
inside the pink sari.

When my brother passed his exam

my parents thanked Ganesha
for the sturdy mental strength
he'd been gifted
Ganesha
decorated in intricate embroidery
riding that tiny mouse
omen of good luck for my brother
who hopes to go to medical school
someday open a clinic.

When bad winds come
when life throws us a dry bone
when the yard dries up
when we are lost for protection
my parents call upon Hanuman
chant his name
call up his physical strength
till we know we are more than
chipped glass, the torn sunset

till the world spits out
more than beggarly
turns moist.

My mother tells me

that Vishnu likes her orderliness
the way she sweeps and tends
wipes down counters
flavors the rice
spices the tandoori chicken
keeps my father resonate
inside the salt of her kisses

that Lakshmi has tutored her
on secret arts
how to flavor the home
fan bight the embers
raise holy the children

candle lamp every room
with gold prosperity.

My father's voice is a soft wing

feathers the gold and blue silk
of my mother's body
that is compact
crowded with prayers

makes her rise early a.m.
special his breakfast
hand roll the chapati
double spice the tikka masala.

For over 35 years
they have learned each other's ways
what makes for impatience
what constitutes respect
which relatives to tender
who to avoid
for what to make room

have been together
every since the arranged marriage
elaborate wedding ceremony
ever since she agreed to leave
her childhood friends
brother and sisters, parents
follow him to a new country.

My father's voice dusts the day
with the tang of cinnamon
coats her heart

for him
she would stand up to a harsh wind
sweep back the dark
snatch the bird of paradise
for him
make it sing.

For the meal

we crush cardamom
prepare the nan bread
biryani
lay out dried figs
lassi, palm wine

I smooth my body
as if it is a blank slate
to be scribed with henna
made ornate

sanctified
in your name.

The crescent moon

does not sleep
keeps guardian over the cassava
the plantains, maize

keeps guardian over my heart
that is tissue thin
perishable
a chipped vase
blue ellipsis

keeps guardian
while the voice of the sarangi
echoes through the hall

calls me out of hiding
stickers my lips moist
to your daybreak.

I have lived here

most of my life
on the other side of the mountain
tutored in want
of your sacred grove

have had ceremonial rice
tossed over my head
witnessed funerals
weddings

suppered with prayer
my parents' over diligent hands
my schoolmates misgivings.

I cup salt
offer it up
to your gold papered altar

as if I can defy greed
become more than a merchant

as if inside the sentience
of your shadow
we are enough.

Shiva

the auspicious one
unchangeable
you call from over the garden wall
wake the birds from slumber

call my heart
that is sometimes a broken vowel
swarm of locust

calm the dogs
cultivate the rice
turn the farmer's field from ruin

come to me
come to me
a slippage of the moon
your consummate
third eye burning.

You spread seed

raise the sugarcane
the maize
the soybeans
raise our hearts

holy the cow
holy the monkey
holy the rat

lend us feet to float
over dust, parched fields
douse with water

blue harmonium our wants
lure them

till we become servants
of wind, emerald
henna the day

turn silence
into the landscape
of larks.

Harvest time

the month of Kartik.
At dawn I drink water
eat nuts, mathri
afterwards abstain
until moonrise
bow low, quiet
make room for the ancestors
a blessing

make room for the one
who comes different
slow turns sorrow
scents the Ashoka tree
fragrant

scents my newborn plumage
till I cannot sleep
fan Parvati in her pampered bed
help her protect
spin the universe golden.

In the grove of sacred trees

under mahogany branches
my lover waits
swollen with figs
agile verses

all night among the peacocks
the sky's dim lamp
I lay with him
on a silken sheet

unlace words
remember our ancestors
birthplace

all night Shiva lounges
gazes over the earth's brown skin
fertilizes
the sorghum

sends Parvati kisses
bright as gemstones
bright as our love.

Around my neck

a serpent lingers
clear eyed
emerald scaled

and in the river of the Ganges
you ripple
rise out of the sediment
your drumbeat
call my name

as if I am holy
the one who sees
the one gone blind

the Gulmohar tree
alive with flame
blossoms.

Off in the distance

a voice calls to me
the day wakes in a field of maize

off in the village
time slurs
the sound of an harmonium
seeps from a ruined doorway

Lakshmi unrolls her bolts of silk
dresses her arms
in a bribe of bracelets

dust to dust
birth to birth

this is what I have been taught
by you

recite prayer
listen
write verse
listen.

Adira Naidu has a degree in biology.
She lives outside Philadelphia with her husband
and two small children.
This is her first chapbook.

www.ingramcontent.com/pod-product-compliance
Lightning Source LLC
Chambersburg PA
CBHW021134080526
44587CB00012B/1281